Emotional Assault:
Recognizing the Abusive Partner's Bag of Tricks

By Lisa Kroulik

Copyright © 2013 Lisa Kroulik
All rights reserved.

ISBN: 1482704897
ISBN-13: 9781482704891

DEDICATION

To my beautiful husband, Darrell, who helped heal my broken heart by showing me what it feels like to be treasured and loved unconditionally. I love you so very much, Darrell, and I still don't know what I did to deserve you. The companionship we have means everything to me.

To the two precious daughters who were born during my first marriage. I am protecting their hearts by not letting them know about this book, but I hope they know that they come first, and I make every decision with their well-being in mind. They are beautiful young ladies who make me proud every day.

To my dear friend, Monica, who was the first person to use the words "manipulative" and "controlling" to describe my ex-husband's behavior. It had simply never occurred to me that the way he treated me might be the problem. She spent countless hours helping me through some of the darkest times in my life, and she empowered me more than she will ever know.

And to the hurting people reading this book. Life can get better, but first you have to understand what is happening and make the decision to change it. I am happy to pass these tools on to you, and I hold you in my heart and prayers.

PREFACE
Meeting and Marrying an Emotional Abuser

More than twenty years ago, I met a man who seemed to have all of the qualities I wanted in a partner. In his dating profile, he described himself as an artist with good morals. He attended church regularly and didn't drink, swear, or smoke. This was a far cry from the type of men I had known prior to meeting him. I also couldn't help but notice that he was tall and handsome. I was smitten with him by the end of our first date.

He seemed to be a really nice, shy, twenty-six-year-old guy without much dating experience. He was a dream come true, and I simply couldn't believe that someone so seemingly perfect would want anything to do with me. My past was troubled, whereas he seemed to be perpetually happy. I fell head-over-heels in love. What I wouldn't understand for at least a decade was that the person I loved never really existed. I was merely in love with an image that he presented to the world. Very few people got to see what this man was really about once the mask was off.

There were issues right from the start, but I always liked to give people the benefit of the doubt. He didn't want to see me more than once a week and always seemed to be involved in his own interests. The activities he enjoyed, such as woodworking and drawing, were not ones that I could participate in with him. While everyone needs solitary pursuits and healthy alone time, I felt like an afterthought. I almost broke up with him several times during our first year together because of it.

I remember him once telling me that it was sometimes a sacrifice to spend time with me because there were so many other things he could be doing. That comment hurt me deeply because I certainly didn't feel that way about him. He was my first priority, and I wanted to spend all of my free time with him. In retrospect, I can see that red flags were there from the beginning but I ignored them. That is why I now counsel anyone who asks to never, ever ignore your own intuition.

A pattern developed early in our relationship. He would say something that confused or hurt me, and I would say nothing about it. I assumed that I was too sensitive and that he didn't really mean anything by his comments and lack of attention toward me. Through it all, he was always nice. He never raised his voice, and he was never physically inappropriate. It would be a long time before I understood the difference between a nice person and a good one. I also knew nothing about narcissistic personality disorder at the time, but now when I look back, I see evidence of the condition. However, my book isn't going to be about narcissism. Rather, it is about the myriad tricks used by emotionally abusive people to gain and retain control over others.

I was twenty-four when I met this person and twenty-seven when I married him. We were married for thirteen years before our marriage ended in 2008. It was only in the last few years of our marriage and the first few years after the divorce that I realized I had spent sixteen years of my life with someone who was selfish to the core of his being. I learned to identify the many ways he manipulated me and tried to maintain control in the relationship, albeit in a passive-aggressive manner. It was a painful epiphany to realize that he probably never genuinely loved me. I fed his ego and helped him maintain an image. That is what he loved.

Pain with a Purpose

In early 2011, I began to write online articles about emotionally abusive relationships. I often used my own dysfunctional first marriage as an example. The articles have been very well-received. Of all the articles I wrote, the ones about emotional abuse account for about two-thirds of my online traffic. They have been viewed over two hundred thousand times in two years. I find this both sad and rewarding. It's sad that so many people are living with the pain of emotional abuse in their marriages or another intimate relationship. It's also rewarding because people connect with my articles on a deep level. They finally know that they are not crazy and they are not alone.

I have been contacted by dozens of women thanking me for putting their experience into words. Many of these courageous women have since become my friends. Although I may never meet them, we have a connection because of our shared experiences. I have also heard from men, both those who were emotionally abused by a partner and those who recognized themselves in my words. Emotional abuse is a gender-neutral problem.

The more articles I wrote, the more I realized that my ex-husband had an entire arsenal of emotionally abusive tactics to keep me confused, dependent, and scared. In my mind's eye, I could picture someone standing there with a sack, ready to throw his emotional abuse at me until something stuck. I somewhat sarcastically refer to this as the emotional abuser's "bag of tricks."

If he had to, my ex would use them all: sulking and silent treatments, projection, character attacks, blaming, shaming, playing the victim, re-writing history, denial, gas-lighting, playing dumb, temper tantrums, and more. Naming the behaviors was incredibly helpful; it allowed me to understand how my ex-husband operates. It dawned on me that I could reach out to many more confused and hurting people by publishing a book about the emotional artillery used by abusers.

And with that, let me introduce you to the emotional abuser's bag of tricks. I use examples from my own life for each trick in order to make it more understandable. While you may not have experienced the same situations, having a concrete example will hopefully help you understand the many different forms of emotional manipulation. Always remember that knowledge is power. People in intimate relationships disagree all the time, sometimes strongly so. However, that doesn't give either person the right to play dirty. By the time you are done reading this book, you may realize that the two of you aren't even playing the same game.

PART I

Trick #1:
The Silent Treatment

Let's say that two six-year-old children are playing a game and a dispute breaks out because one of them feels that the other is not following the rules. The one making the accusations stomps off, arms folded across his chest. "I'm not talking to you!" he declares. The bewildered playmate is sad and wonders what she did to make her friend treat her like this. She doesn't remember breaking any rules and just wants her friend back. Childhood squabbles being what they are, the incident is quickly forgotten and the game resumes.

Now imagine the above scenario again, but this time the players are a husband and wife who have been together for sixteen years. The issue at hand is more serious than a board game, but the childish behavior is exactly the same. The husband is playing the part of the angry child who walks away and won't communicate, while the wife is just hurt and confused. I don't have to imagine it because I lived it. Welcome to the sad, lonely, and confusing world of living with someone who uses the silent treatment as a method of control. I am listing this abusive tactic first because it is the one that my ex-husband used most frequently and the one that hurt me the most. I call this type of person a stonewaller.

Stonewalling and the silent treatment both refer to the actions of a person wishing to convey his displeasure with you by refusing to speak to or look at you, leaving the room when you enter it, or speaking to others in the room while ignoring you. In my case, my ex-husband could exhibit all of these behaviors for several consecutive days. The tension in our home was unbearable, and our two young daughters took it all in. He would talk and laugh with them like a normal father while turning his back on me as if I didn't exist.

More often than not, his stonewalling didn't stop until I apologized for what I would perceive to be my shortcoming. He would never tell me what I had done to supposedly offend him so much. If I asked, I only got ice-cold silence and a glare in return. I would be emotionally devastated because I just wanted to communicate to resolve the problem. He could hold out until he broke me, and that was exactly his goal. By the end of a prolonged silent treatment, I would be so physically and emotionally exhausted that I just said what he wanted to hear in order for it to end.

The stonewaller may not say anything verbally, but his actions clearly express the anger and aggressiveness he is feeling within. Rather than promoting open communication between spouses to resolve differences, the stonewaller turns the situation into a power struggle. To him, it is all about winning. If he pouts and refuses to talk to his partner, she will eventually become exasperated enough to drop whatever issue she was trying to address. In this way, he manipulates her into doing exactly what he wants. In my case, that was to never bring up problems or expect accountability from him. I was also never to question his extreme selfishness or sense of entitlement.

For the One Who Is Being Ignored

The partner of a stonewaller can't survive long-term without suffering serious repercussions to her own mental health. I struggled with severe depression because I knew things were terribly wrong in our marriage. We could never discuss our issues, and so I assumed that I was the problem. I lived in constant fear of saying the wrong thing and being subjected to days of the silent treatment as punishment. I was very serious and rarely smiled. He never said the words, but I certainly got the message that he must always get his own way.

However, not too many people could see through him or guess how we really lived. My ex-husband was not only a stonewaller but a narcissist as well. Like all narcissists, he could be charming and would stop at nothing to bolster his public persona as an all-around good guy. The majority of people in our lives believed it, including me because I had not yet identified his narcissism and all its traits as the root of our problems. I perpetually berated myself for being unhappy and wondered what in the world was wrong with me. I mean, I was married to such a nice guy, and he was so patient to put up with me. Oh, how I roll my eyes at the way I used to think.

My anxiety over our relationship was not limited to my waking hours. Panic attacks would grip me in the middle of the night. I would wake up with a racing heart, gasping for air, sure that I was a few seconds from death. However, what was worse than the anxiety was the confusion that comes from living with an emotional abuser. You're never sure of what is true because he determines your reality. In spite of the fact that my ex-husband never laid a hand on me in anger, my behavior around him resembled that of a physically abused person. Psychological and physical abuse can trigger the same survival instincts in its victims.

Why Stonewalling Hurts so Much

Everyone needs to be loved unconditionally and to feel validated. Your spouse is supposed to love you more than anyone else. When he deliberately ignores you, it says that you are just not that important. Marriages can't survive this type of emotional battery. Over time, it erodes intimacy, trust, and happiness within the relationship. If the two of you decide to salvage the relationship, the stonewaller must be willing to submit to intensive counseling in order to understand what drives his deep need to control. He must also be committed to making changes in the way he communicates with his spouse. The relationship needs to be a give-and-take one, and the need to control can never enter the equation.

This did not happen in my first marriage. The changes my ex-husband attempted were superficial and only to appease me. On a deeper level, he did not understand how his own behavior was destroying our relationship. After several rounds of therapy on both of our parts, nothing had really changed. He still employed the silent treatment tactic whenever he was upset with me. In the final months of our marriage, more days than not were filled with total silence. I began to dread him coming home and would plan to be out of the house whenever possible. I needed to be around people who recognized that I was an important person with thoughts and opinions of my own. On a typical day, within thirty seconds of him coming home I knew how he would treat me the rest of the evening. His mood—and my reaction to it—set the tone for our entire family.

Something inside of me snapped during the last episode of stonewalling. I was physically, emotionally, and spiritually spent. I could not last another day being treated like that. Marriage is supposed to be a partnership, but I lived with an overgrown child who demanded that he be catered to and who made my life a living hell when I didn't see things his way. It was a horrible example for our two children, and that is what finally gave me the courage to leave.

If you are in a relationship with someone who uses the stonewalling strategy, know that it is emotional manipulation, and it is not normal or healthy. Some of the excuses you may hear include that

- he just needed to blow off steam,
- he didn't want to argue, or
- you were too hysterical to listen to reason anyway.

Not speaking to your spouse for days is not blowing off steam. It is punishment, pure and simple. If you want the relationship to survive, the person who stonewalls must be willing to get help. If he refuses, you need to decide if the behavior is something that you can live with or not. In my situation, it literally took a physical breakdown for me to see that my ex-husband regularly engaged in psychological torture. Even so, it took another fifteen months of soul-searching to make the decision to end the marriage.

I am not in a position to give people advice one way or the other. I just know from experience that living with an emotionally manipulative person is confusing and overwhelming. My only desire is to give you the awareness you need to make an informed decision on your own.

Trick #2:
Turning the Tables

I could never understand the lengths my ex-husband would go to in order to not discuss, and thereby avoid any attempt to resolve, his own issues. His defense mechanisms were ridiculous then, and they are ridiculous now. Before going into the total shutdown mode of stonewalling, he would often first try to throw me off balance by countering anything I would say with something very minor that he "had" on me. I have two classic examples that illustrate what I refer to as "spin control" or "tit for tat."

When I tried to discuss something that confused or upset me, nearly every one of his sentences started with, "But what about what you've done?"

The Truck Incident

Although we were deeply in debt, my ex decided that he should have a brand new truck. He was driving a truck that was probably twelve years old at the time, and he had been talking for a while about replacing it. One of his first comments when I totaled my van a year earlier was, "That puts my truck plans on the back burner." He said nothing about the fact that our oldest daughter and I were unharmed in the accident. She was only eight years old at the time.

We discussed his desire to replace his truck very briefly one weekend. I commented that after my accident, I had to charge the down payment for my next car on our credit card because we had no savings. A few days after this discussion, he called after being gone all day on a Saturday and told me he had purchased a brand new truck. But that was not the shock. I asked him how much he had spent, and he calmly told me over $31,000. He informed me that he had put the down payment for his new truck on our credit card, just as I had told him to do. That is sure not how I remember the conversation.

He went on to say that I gave him my blessing to buy any truck that he wanted. I cringe when I look back and see the obvious manipulation now that I am several years removed from the situation. Also cringeworthy is how he insisted that I told him to put the down payment on a credit card and gave him my blessing to be completely irresponsible. Emotional abusers are awesome at rewriting history and manipulating your emotions in order to suit their own needs.

I told him that I had said no such things and that we couldn't afford truck payments that were now going to be $415 a month for the next six years. He skipped over that and went right to, "Well, what about your car? That costs money too." Really, Ex, was that the best you could come up with? Bringing up a car I had to buy when my previous vehicle was destroyed in an accident? A car that we actually discussed and agreed on? A car that cost less than one-third of the truck?

I should have seen it coming, but I didn't. That is how I was manipulated into defending my purchase of an absolutely necessary vehicle for the rest of the conversation. He had succeeded at turning the tables in the conversation and focusing on how much my vehicle had cost. Never mind that I didn't sneak out behind his back to buy it the way he did to me.

The shock and confusion I felt in this situation is best described as someone pulling the carpet out from underneath you. You didn't even see anyone standing there to yank it away, yet now you are left lying on the ground and trying to figure out where the attack came from. It leaves you in a state of hyper-alertness because you are waiting for the next unforeseen attack.

The Decades-Old Porn Addiction He Failed to Mention

After ten years of marriage and thirteen years together, I discovered that my ex had a serious pornography addiction, which predated our relationship. He was spending hundreds of dollars a month to get his fix—money that we just didn't have. We lived in a run-down house and didn't have health insurance; our money could have been better spent on those things. Although I was devastated and felt betrayed, I was willing to stick with him if he agreed to get help. I told him that he had a serious addiction and that counseling was non-negotiable.

At this point, the ex was gracious enough to point out that I had an addiction as well. Yep, I sure did. My addiction was to Diet Pepsi. In his mind, lying to me for over a decade was comparable to my caffeine fixes that got me through the day. Even back then, when I was so sickly co-dependent, I had to laugh. He knew he was busted, and so he spun it around to make it about my caffeine consumption. My heart was shattered into pieces, but that didn't matter as long as he could make me look just as bad. Really, what kind of person does that to people he is supposed to love?

I wish I could say it got better, but the tit for tat behavior has only gotten more ridiculous since we've been divorced. When I recently reported him for being three months behind in child support, he responded by accusing me of starving our children. A police officer came to our home to make sure there was enough food for our two girls because their father was terribly concerned about it. Interestingly, he was never concerned before I turned him in for being a deadbeat dad.

Standing Up to an Emotional Bully

It takes unflinching determination to stand up to this kind of behavior. To be honest, it's downright exhausting at times. Once I figured out what my ex was up to, I repeatedly tried to go back to the topic at hand when he would use this tactic against me. Unfortunately, I was dealing with a master of spin control. He simply ignored whatever I was trying to discuss and dug up anything he could to throw me off balance. It didn't matter how ludicrous or painful it was. If he was really in the doghouse, he would go after my most vulnerable areas until I was too upset to continue the conversation.

If necessary, repeat yourself like a broken record until the other person gets the message that you see right through the manipulative behavior. He may not stop, but at least he knows that you're on to him. Be warned, though: this strategy will probably cause the offensive behavior to get worse. It may even lead you to decide whether or not you should remain in the relationship. Sometimes, it's easier to pretend everything is fine rather than face that decision. I know; I have been there.

Trick #3:
Poor Me!

A person exhibiting the "Poor Me Syndrome" gets you to believe that you have deeply wounded him in an attempt to take the focus off his own behavior. I had no idea how popular this tactic was until this article got one hundred thousand views in eighteen months. Emotionally abusive people have an uncanny ability to play the victim and get others to feel sorry for them. This leaves you feeling that you have to take care of this person and that you have no right to have any expectations in the relationship. People with co-dependent personalities fall into this type of pattern pretty naturally.

My Best Example

For most of our marriage, I lived in such denial that I could not see my ex's manipulative behavior even when friends pointed it out to me in specific detail. When the mental fog began to clear, I realized I was married to an emotional abuser who had no interest in changing. I filed for divorce in late 2008. My ex used this opportunity to get people at our church to feel sorry for him, even though some of them were aware that his sexual addictions and passive-aggressive behavior were the main causes of our strained relationship. I had been pretty open about our struggles because I desperately wanted to keep our marriage together.

A church member whom I had become somewhat close to heard that we were getting a divorce and asked him why. With the most contrived, wounded expression on his face that he could drum up and tears brimming in the corners of his eyes, he told her we were splitting up because "she just won't forgive me." What he failed to mention was that I had caught him trolling the Internet and looking for dates on a very sexually explicit website. The concerned church member cornered me and let me have it for hurting my husband so much. I laughed and let her know that she had just seen the act of a brilliant narcissist and had fallen for it hook, line, and sinker. It seemed to have never occurred to her that he could be lying.

The Motive Behind Their Ploys for Sympathy

The whole reason behind why people engage in this kind of behavior can be summed up in two words: image management. People who play the victim are not usually emotionally in tune with themselves enough to recognize the offense and hurt they cause others. Instead, they tend to see themselves as a morally righteous victim.

Since they are unable to tolerate any hint to the contrary, they quickly turn the tables and find a way to elicit sympathy from others. While operating in Poor Me mode, abusers don't generally rely on other types of manipulative behavior like verbal attacks and projection. It is hard to feel sorry for someone when he's acting like a jerk. These people are emotional predators who know that it pains normal people to see others suffer. They zero in on this and throw a pity party until the other person relents and says, yes, maybe I am the problem after all. It is just one of many tricks an abuser uses to avoid being held responsible for his own behavior.

They Look to Exploit Your Vulnerabilities

In order to get their own needs met, emotionally abusive people tend to latch onto mates who are especially vulnerable and need to take care of others to feel worthwhile. Abusers have a deep need to control others, and so they will pick out someone who is the most likely to go along with it. In an intimate relationship, the abuser plays the victim to get the other person to feel as if she is to blame for his unhappiness.

My ex, for example, would frequently ask me, "Why are you doing this to me?" when I tried to put forth my expectations of change so our marriage would survive. It had the desired effect: he got me to back off and feel guilty for even suggesting that he needed to change. It also caused me to look elsewhere for the cause of our discord and to surmise that I must be the one with the problem. That was exactly how he wanted it.

How to Know When You Are Being Manipulated

It can be very difficult to realize that someone is taking advantage of you, especially when it is by someone you know well and love. This may be the way you have always interacted, and so it can be hard to start calling someone on his behavior. The thing about living in close proximity with an emotional abuser is that your mind can become clouded and your thinking distorted.

- If the same scenarios seem to continuously resurface, someone who is not as close to the situation may be able to help you see things more objectively.
- If you catch someone in the act of trying to play the victim, let him know what you see.

I recall waking up one morning to a note from my ex that said, "I do nothing but hurt you (and our daughters) and would be better off hanging myself in the garage." Now, I am not suggesting that all threats of suicide are only ploys to emotionally manipulate someone, but I knew exactly what he was doing. Narcissists think far too highly of themselves to actually commit suicide. I told him to stop it. The note happened to come after a particularly rough exchange the night before in which I had let out all of the hurt I had kept to myself for years. His response was to threaten suicide in an attempt to get me to feel sorry for him and never express a negative emotion again. This illustrates how his sympathy was not for me but for himself. My emotional pain was never even acknowledged.

With some perspective and a chance to clear your mind, it is usually easy to see right through the tactics the emotionally abusive person uses. If someone is trying to play the victim with you, remind yourself that you are not responsible for anyone else's happiness. It is healthy to emotionally detach and let that person know that he alone controls his well-being. Stop the abuser in his tracks by letting him know you see what is going on and you will not tolerate it. This may sound like a terrifying proposition after putting up with it for so many years, but I assure you that it is very liberating and a necessary step in breaking free from abuse and getting your life back.

Trick #4:
You're Not Perfect Either!

I would like to take this opportunity to let my readers know that I am an imperfect human being. I know this will come as a major shock to you. I am overweight and too emotional, for starters. I tend to react very poorly to stress and often act before I have had a chance to think things through. Before I gave into the desire to write for a living, I bounced from job to job because I got bored so easily. I am telling you this in the interest of full disclosure. It is also an automatic reaction on my part after living with an emotionally abusive husband for thirteen years. No one should think that I am trying to make myself look perfect! I will expand on that in a moment. I think most people, with the exception of people who have delusions of grandeur, accept the fact that they are not perfect. I certainly do.

How Dare You Expect Me to Change?

My ex got angry during any conversation that included my thoughts about something he did to upset me. The conversation would inevitably deteriorate into him accusing me of thinking I am perfect. He would then go on to list several ways I fall short of perfection. Although we went to church every Sunday, I never heard him quote scripture unless he was trying to defend himself. Matthew 7:3 was a particular favorite: "Why do you look at the speck of sawdust in your brother's eye when you pay no attention to the plank in your own eye?" His tone was always righteous and condemning, making me feel awful that I said anything about him when I have so many faults of my own. What is ironic about this is that his issue was usually the log in the eye and mine was the speck by comparison.

The First Cousin of Projection

Pulling the "you're not perfect" card is somewhat similar to projection. The major difference between projection and pointing out how imperfect you are is that when using projection, the abusive person ascribes to you a fault that is actually one of his own flaws. For example, my ex can hold a grudge like nobody's business. That is why he frequently accused me of doing the same thing, even though I gave him more chances than any sane person would. Abusers soothe their own guilty conscience by telling themselves that they are not hurting you and that you are the one hurting them. However, some abusive people have no conscience and simply project onto you for their own amusement.

The abuser points out that you're not perfect in order to make you feel guilt and to prevent any form of resolution to your conflict. The abusive person may have a legitimate issue with you, or he may just make something up to throw you off track. I know it sounds crazy, but you may find yourself apologizing by the end of the conservation. He will expect you to beg his forgiveness for bringing up his fault, all while he is shaming you for your own shortcomings.

Why Yes, I Do Have an Example

My ex never liked my family, and there was some major conflict with them during the last several months of our marriage. It was a horrible position for me to be in because I love my family and I still loved him. I just wanted them to get along. I pushed him to apologize for the way he treated them and to try to improve several relationships. He informed me that my family—including my parents, stepparents, siblings, in-laws, nieces, and nephews—just didn't excite him. I was also told that they "rub me the wrong way." My ex accused me of loving them more than him and thinking they were perfect. Naturally, this also meant that I thought I was perfect, and I needed to leave my ex alone.

I turned around and did the same thing to my family that he did to me. I pointed out their most painful mistakes and defended my ex's antisocial behavior. Little by little, staying with him meant losing other people in my life because I had to defend my decision to remain in the marriage. I could not see things any differently than he told me to see them. He was always the victim, and my family and friends simply disliked him for no good reason.

There's the Tit for Tat Again

It doesn't take long to realize that many of these emotionally abusive tactics overlap. It was inevitable that my ex would sidetrack any issue with a fault of mine, many of which I never knew I had. During the conflict with my family, I learned that I embarrassed him when we would go out to eat because I "slop" on my clothes. Boy, did that make me feel stupid and put me in my place for being imperfect. However, I wondered why he had never brought it up before if my restaurant eating habits had been embarrassing him for sixteen years. I saw that he was scraping the bottom of the barrel to find my speck of dust while at the same time ignoring his plank of being consistently rude to my family.

Interestingly, his mother responds with the "you're not perfect either" line whenever a problem is brought to her attention. When I sought her help to speak to him about his past-due child support, she ignored me. Like her son, every issue is someone else's fault and image is more important than substance or truth. After she received my e-mail, she called her son and told him I said the kids were starving. It took some pretty creative interpretation to come up with that statement. What I actually said was that they are not starving, thanks to the financial support of me and their stepfather. However, I still expected my ex to meet his obligations as their biological father.

Between the two of them, my former mother-in-law and my ex decided that my husband and I are neglecting the kids. My ex-husband contacted the local police department and asked them to do a child welfare check. It took the responding officer less than 30 seconds to see that the claim was bogus. The officer told me that former spouses frequently involve the police to get back at each other, and I confirmed that is exactly what had happened here. I got my ex's message loud and clear: I will humiliate you if you try to hold me accountable.

How to Deal with Your Imperfection

It is extremely frustrating to attempt to have an adult conversation with someone who resorts to pointing out that you're not perfect because he refuses to acknowledge his own defects. You can try to address the concern without getting sidetracked from the original issue. "I realize that I am not perfect. However, that is not what I am trying to discuss here. Please give me the courtesy of hearing my concerns without becoming defensive. If you have concerns about me, I would be happy to hear them in another conversation." Your message may get through if the other person truly does not see the error of his ways and genuinely wants your relationship to work.

Unfortunately, emotional abusers only want relationships to work on their terms. In that case, you can expect the abusive behavior to escalate when you call him out on it. Even if you hear his concerns and try to correct your shortcomings, he will always come up with another one. After a while, you may realize that he does not truly love you at all. He simply loves being able to control you.

Trick #5:
Rewriting History

Wouldn't it be nice to go back in time and be able to change events to make yourself look better? Who wouldn't go for that? Apparently, this is an offer that emotional abusers just can't refuse. Since accepting responsibility or committing to changing their behavior is out of the question, the next best thing is to travel back in time and change the way events unfolded in the first place. When this happens in political circles, it's referred to as revisionism. When it happens enough in relationships, it can make the other person feel like she is going insane. Psychologists refer to this little trick as rewriting history.

That's Not the Way It Happened at All

In tip #4, I talked about the difficult relationship between my ex-husband and nearly every member of my extended family—about twenty-five people. He thought he was too good for any of them. The admission that they just didn't excite him and that they rubbed him the wrong way didn't come out until the last months of our marriage. Prior to that, he would attempt to discredit my family members by insisting that one of them had said something rude to him. The statements changed frequently until he finally gave up and admitted he just didn't like them—or people in general, for that matter. However, I found this behavior maddening while we were still together. His version of events kept changing, and it made me question my own sanity.

After our divorce, I checked with several members of my family to see if any of it was true. Of course it wasn't. Rather than admit he was antisocial, he rolled several tricks into one to avoid having anything to do with my family. He rewrote history, projected his own issues onto them, and made himself out to be the victim. Several family members told me about rude comments he made about them when I was not present.

For example, I begged him to help my mother and stepfather move a piece of furniture one Saturday. Other people in the family were always willing to help, and his refusal embarrassed me, especially because he claimed to be a Christian. He begrudgingly did it and then told my mother and stepfather that he had to leave because he had better things to do. I guess that was a favorite line of his.

My ex was always aloof and looked bored at my family gatherings. My brother attempted to make conservation with him by asking for his advice about a home project he was going to do. It just so happened to be in the same line of work that my ex-husband was in. My ex blew up at my brother and accused him of wanting free labor. I didn't know about either of these incidents, and several others like them, until after I was away from this man. Talk about rewriting history to make himself look like an upstanding person. What I find sad now is that I bought it, and it alienated me from people who actually did love me. The loneliness I felt was absolutely crushing at times.

I Don't Remember Saying That

If I had a nickel for every time my ex-husband said he didn't remember saying something that I clearly remembered him saying, well, I'd have a lot of nickels by now. By the end of our marriage, I remember threatening to buy a tape recorder just so I could prove that I was neither crazy nor hard of hearing. It didn't matter if he had made the statement in question just minutes earlier, he would still deny saying it if I pressed him on it or it made him look bad. When someone does this to you enough, you start to wonder if maybe he is right.

I don't know how he could lie with such a straight face. It is one of the many talents of narcissists and other personality-disordered individuals. He would be completely sincere when he claimed that he did not remember a promise he made or a hurtful statement.

Another term for this type of behavior is gaslighting. The abusive person distorts your reality so often that you begin to doubt yourself. Did I just hear that? No, it must be my imagination. My partner would never say such a thing to me. Gaslighting is controlling behavior at its finest.

According to Wikipedia, gaslighting is defined as "A form of psychological abuse in which false information is presented with the intent of making the victim doubt his memory, perception, and sanity. Instances may range from simple denial that previous instances ever occurred, up to staging bizarre events by the abuser with the intention of disorienting the victim." I love the use of the word "disorienting." That is exactly what it feels like to live with someone who regularly engages in psychological bullying.

The term gaslighting is taken from the 1938 play *Gas Light*, in which the antagonist tries to drive his victim crazy by taking things from the house and then denying they are gone.

When in Doubt, Document

Your sanity is something worth fighting for.

- If your partner regularly describes past events in ways you know are false, write down the events the way you remember them.
- You may also want to write down what other people have said about past situations.
- For conversations in the present, recording them is not a bad idea. You may have to go undercover to pull this one off, but you will have proof of what was actually said.
- If you aren't comfortable acting sneaky like that, consider letting your partner know that you plan to buy a special pen and journal. When he says something questionable, hold up your hand as if to say, "Stop!" You can then let him know that you are writing down exactly what he just said. This may make him so uncomfortable that he reconsiders his behavior. It may also cause him to do the same to you, whether there is justification for it or not.

Trick #6:
But I'm a Really Good Person

This little trick is similar to playing the victim, but it is a little different because it always comes with an air of righteousness. The abusive person acts deeply offended when you point out behavior that you find questionable. Your concerns are piously dismissed while the abuser prepares to do what he does best: turn the situation around and make you believe you are the one with the problem. As usual, my best example of this behavior comes from my personality-disordered ex-husband.

When our marriage finally died the death that it should have experienced years earlier, the ex decided he was not going to spend any more money on housing than necessary. He got a studio apartment and still lives there more than four years later. That would be lovely if he was a swinging bachelor or a college student, but we have two girls, who were twelve and nine years old when we got divorced. The original visitation plan had the girls spending Fridays overnight with their father, but there was no way I was going to allow them to all sleep in the same small room together. The one and only time I have been in his apartment was when I was evaluating the possibility of overnights for the girls.

When I questioned my ex-husband about his living arrangement and informed him that I would not allow the girls to stay overnight unless they had a separate bedroom, he was incredulous. What was wrong with me? How could I think that he would hurt his girls? He would build a partition if it would make me happy. Four and a half years later, there is no partition and the girls have yet to stay overnight at their dad's apartment.

Did you notice that I never accused him of wanting to hurt our girls? I simply thought there could be a more appropriate sleeping arrangement than for pubescent girls to sleep with or very close to their father.

When she was twelve, our youngest girl went away for the weekend with her dad, his girlfriend, and his girlfriend's teenage son. Can you guess what the sleeping arrangements looked like? Two unmarried people who claimed to be righteous Christians were in one room while our daughter and the girlfriend's son were in another. As usual, he ignored my concerns and told our daughter I was overreacting. For her part, the girlfriend swore at me and told me I had a dirty mind.

The Mask of Righteousness

To this day, many people believe that my ex-husband is an absolutely wonderful person. It is extremely awkward to run into someone who doesn't know that we split up more than four years ago and who doesn't know the real story. The person looks shocked and confused when I say that we are divorced. He or she saw a nice, church-going guy who appeared to love his family. What could possibly have happened? I usually get looked at like there must be something terribly wrong with me for letting him go. I'm not saying I am perfect or blameless, but to be looked at like I am crazy is not a pleasant experience.

The whole "righteous" routine can be particularly nauseating if the abusive person hides behind his faith. As far as I know, my ex-husband has missed very few Sunday services throughout his life. I didn't pursue the Christian faith until after I met him and have always been honest about my struggles. After my ex and I split up, I leaned heavily on my faith and believe that God led me toward the blessed existence I know today. My ex-husband, on the other hand, felt that he had the right answer and that anyone who disagreed with him was going to hell. While I wrestled with what I truly believe and tried to grow as a person, he told me that he was fine the way he was. "I'm not like you. I don't need to grow."

About three years before we divorced, I started taking our children, who were eight and five at the time, to a church that had radically different beliefs than the one we had been attending with their father. The ex made no effort to stop me and didn't seem worried that (in his mind) his children were apparently going to hell right along with me. As far as he was concerned, he had it right and that was all that mattered. My ex would justify his apathy by telling people that he couldn't change my mind anyway. Maybe not, but to condemn his own children to hell while proclaiming to be the perfect Christian still boggles my mind. The people at church saw him as a patient, loving husband who was waiting for his wife to return to the fold.

Confronting False Superiority

If there is one thing that narcissists and the personality disordered don't have, it's humility. Quite simply, they are right and everyone else is wrong. Unfortunately, it's nearly impossible for people who don't deal with an emotional abuser day in and day out to see this. They believe the mask. For years my ex's boss thought the world revolved around my ex. I think the mask was starting to crack, so he just got a new job and a new boss.

From my experience, I learned the one thing that makes emotionally abusive people angrier than anything else is to suggest that they are not the righteous people they claim to be. This is when the personal attacks on you can get vicious. I would like to say that I know my ex's cruel words are ridiculous and that they don't hurt me, but I would be lying. He still has the ability to wound me deeply, especially when he insinuates that I am a bad mother.

- If you decide to confront your partner, be prepared for the potential onslaught.

In my case, I became increasingly disgusted by the difference between his public behavior and the way he treated my family and me in private. It was a huge disconnect, and, like every other aspect of living with him, it was very disorienting. I couldn't pretend anymore that he was a good person.

If you find yourself in this situation, I hope you will take the words of author Alice Walker to heart: "No person is your friend who demands your silence or denies your right to grow."

Trick #7:
You're Not Very Forgiving

In case you haven't picked up on it by now, let me state it again: emotional abusers are big on deflecting shame onto others. Who wants to be told he or she is not a forgiving person? Just hearing those words makes most people feel deeply ashamed. When you throw in the fact that both people are supposed to be Christians, it makes the situation even worse. My ex used this trick fairly often, and he really laid it on thick as our marriage was falling apart.

Wow, You Really Hold a Grudge

I experienced several traumatic events during my early years that were difficult for me to overcome. When the memories resurfaced, I looked to my then-husband for comfort and understanding. I got neither. He simply looked at me blankly, as if he had no idea why I was talking about events from so long ago. I got fake empathy exactly one time, but from then on I was expected not to discuss my pain. It didn't even matter that he wasn't the one who caused it. Suffice to say that he never discussed anything of substance either. While I was trying to form an emotional bond with him, all I got was judgment. He told me that I really hold a grudge against people and that I just need to forget about the past.

   I agree that hanging onto the past can be damaging. However, I don't think there is anything healthy about stuffing away painful memories and never discussing them again. Most women need to verbalize their thoughts in order to process what happened to them. Often times, that means discussing the event several times. Sometimes I just needed to cry and have someone give me a hug. I needed to hear that events from my childhood were not my fault. I didn't need to hear that I hold a grudge. That almost hurt more than the original incidents. I didn't expect my ex to be a therapist, but I did expect basic human empathy. Now that I know he is a narcissist, I understand that I expected too much.

You Have a Black Heart

There is no limit to how low these types of people will stoop to make you feel awful about yourself. As long as they can justify their own actions, your emotional pain is of no consequence to them. Case in point: I was told that I am not only unforgiving but that I actually have a black heart. Here is what caused him to say that my heart is discolored.

   A few weeks after my ex-husband moved out, I found an envelope full of receipts for items he bought for his personal porn collection. It appeared that he had been saving them to get a free product. Even though I had seen firsthand evidence of what he was into, finding the receipts was emotionally devastating. They were in sequential order by date, proving to me once again how thoroughly he had duped me for years. I mailed the receipts back to him. After all, it looked as if he would need them if he wanted to receive a free item.

When the soon-to-be-ex received the receipts in the mail, he called my cell phone when he knew I couldn't answer it. He left a rambling message about how I was unforgiving and that he felt sorry for me. It was piousness at its best. He ended the message by informing me of the status of my heart. Apparently it is black and I never even knew it.

No Accountability

While the ex heaped shame and judgment upon me, he didn't subject himself to the same standards. There was no apology for having the receipts in the first place and no acknowledgment of the pain that finding them caused me. I guess it didn't really matter anymore by that point. Unfortunately, I really let his words get to me. When I told my good friend about the black heart comment, she just laughed. She understood his propensity for ridiculous statements all too well. I wished I could have done the same.

The "black-hearted and unforgiving" remark hurt me because it exposed my deepest fear. What if it was true and I ended my marriage just because I couldn't forgive? Yes, I see the foolishness of that thought now, but it bugged me at the time. What if other people thought the same thing about me? My ex knew the statement would bother me, which is exactly why he said it. That is what emotionally abusive people do.

- Abusive people sniff out your vulnerabilities and go in for the kill.

Demanding Your Forgiveness Is Not Love

When I found out about my ex-husband's longstanding pornography habit, it felt like I had gotten the wind knocked out of me. I could not function for days. Instead of giving me space, he demanded to know if I could forgive him. I certainly wanted to, but I needed time to process my intense feelings of shock and betrayal. He moped around the house and occasionally threw some apologetic words my way. Unfortunately, there was very little feeling behind them. I didn't doubt that he was sorry, but it wasn't for hurting me so deeply. He was only sorry that he got caught.

A person who is truly sorry doesn't attach moral judgment to your response. He offers his sincere apologies with no expectations whatsoever. His only motivation is doing the right thing, not judging you for how long it takes you to forgive the offense. Unfortunately, some members of my faith community also heaped shame and judgment on me. I was actually told to forgive him and never bring up the issue of his porn addiction again. His empty "sorry" was supposed to be enough because Christ had forgiven me for my sins. It was insinuated that the future of our marriage rested solely on my ability to forgive, not on my ex taking any responsibility for his actions or changing his behavior. Talk about pressure.

- The bottom line is that no one can demand forgiveness or give you a timetable to get over seriously hurtful behavior.

It is not fair to be judged as unforgiving or bitter. If you are struggling to forgive, seek counseling or talk to a friend you can trust. Always remember that forgiveness is a journey and not a destination. Only you get to decide the path.

Trick #8:
It's All a Misunderstanding and Other Hodgepodge Tricks

The ex, being the perfect specimen that he is, could never admit to making a mistake or hurting me. If I felt hurt by something he said or did, then there must have been a problem with my interpretation. It certainly could not mean that he had done anything wrong. I was typically labeled as being too sensitive, unforgiving, or demanding. Of these, my personal favorite is that I have a "black heart."

When he knew he had to fess up because it turned out that I was a lot smarter than he ever gave me credit for, he would never admit wrongdoing. Instead I was told that it was just a misdeed. We're all sinners, after all. In using this crafty language, he often fell back on trick #4 and accused me of thinking that I'm perfect. My interpretation of an event was never acknowledged as being legitimate. My ex often spoke very formally when responding to the news that he had hurt me. "You misunderstood me. That was not my intent. I apologize." It sounded wooden and rehearsed. However, it was hard to counter when he appeared to be apologetic.

Your Approach Is Wrong

During our marriage, I was desperate to understand the workings of my ex-husband's mind. He went through extensive counseling twice, and we had a few brief stints of couple's counseling. I assumed he would want to share his new insights from counseling with me, and we could help each other grow. How wrong I was. He didn't voluntarily share a single thing. When I would get upset, he faulted my approach. If I wasn't too demanding, unforgiving, or sensitive, then it was just the wrong time. Almost always, he was too tired. Naturally he had plenty of energy for the things he wanted to do.

This was an exasperating way to live. I didn't know how to approach him perfectly so he would discuss issues with me. It took me a long time to see that this was just a smokescreen to distract me. Most emotionally abusive people are incapable of honestly discussing an issue and coming up with a resolution. It would require self-awareness, which they simply don't have. If they reflected inward, they could potentially discover a flaw, and if the abusive person in your life is a narcissist, he can't tolerate even the suggestion that he has any faults. Rest assured, though: he is happy to point out yours.

Nice Guys Can Still Manipulate

My ex-husband loved to envision himself as a nice guy, and so he sometimes asked me what I wanted to do for the day or for the evening. That is, if he decided to grace me with his presence at all. I cried myself to sleep many lonely nights because I longed for him to choose to be with me instead of making it sound as if I forced him to. Believe me, a heart can tell the difference.

On the rare occasion that he could put aside his own interests, he would ask me what I wanted to do during our time together. He would smile and seem genuinely interested in my thoughts on the matter. However, the minute I made a suggestion, he would respond with something like "Are you sure you want to do that?" and give his own suggestion instead. You guessed it: that's usually what we ended up doing. It got to the point where I would tell him to make the plans because he was just going to override me anyway. This little tactic served to make my ex look like a caring husband while still getting his own way.

When All Else Fails, Throw Stuff Around and Act Like a Jerk

My ex was very proud of the fact that he never swore or was physically abusive toward our daughters or me. This is not to say that he wasn't above using physical intimidation when he thought it was necessary. More than once he got within inches of my face and made comments like "Are you sure about that?" to try to intimidate me. He would slam doors, smash the girls' toys when they were in his way, or take off for hours and not tell me where he was going.

I remember once I came home to find my girls crying hysterically in the backyard. Their father could not find the TV remote, and he was screaming at them to find it while he threw couch cushions all over the living room. When our oldest daughter was four, he asked her a question and she didn't respond right away. He pounded his fists on the table and screamed, "Answer me!" right in her face. I took her and her one-year-old sister and left for a day, but I didn't leave for good for another eight years. My reasoning was that he didn't hit us and therefore wasn't abusive.

Animal Abuse

You may have heard that the way a person treats animals can predict how he or she might eventually treat people. If that theory is true, I have even more reason to be grateful that I got the heck out of that marriage. Our first pet was an eight-week-old puppy. I'm not a dog person at all, and so I found housebreaking quite trying. We had had the puppy for a month and he was still having an accident in the house every day. I was at the end of my rope. My ex told me that he would take care of the problem and began to fill the bathtub up with water. Horrified, I asked what he was doing. He planned to drown the puppy. He also said he had swords he could use. I grabbed the dog and headed to the Humane Society. I couldn't stand by while he did that, even though I never learned the puppy's fate after I dropped him off.

Ten years later, we had another dog. She liked to run for it whenever the door was open. The ex was getting tired and frustrated with spending his evenings searching the neighborhood for the dog. He came home one night, furious, with the large coonhound on his shoulders. Once he got in the house, he threw the dog to the floor as hard as he could. Her whimpering broke my heart. In light of that experience, it probably makes sense that she never returned the next time she escaped from the house.

Our cats have fared much better. They are now ten and five years old and are especially attached to my second husband.

And There You Have It

I'm sure my ex-husband displayed many more tricks than this, but I have not lived with him since late 2008, and my memory is thankfully starting to fail me. There are also many more forms of emotional manipulation that others have experienced and I have not.

If you had met me in 2007, I would not have described my ex's behavior in these terms. I distinctly remember telling a friend that he did not have a manipulative bone in his body. I don't know how she kept a straight face. That same friend had the courage to tell me my first husband's behavior was abusive. She then listened to me talk several times a week, sometimes for three or four hours at a time, for the next three years until I figured it out for myself.

- My point here is that it takes time—sometimes lots of it—to see this type of behavior for what it is.

When all you hear is what a terrible person you are, it can be hard to trust your own instincts. This is a mistake. God gave us instincts for a reason, so keep talking until someone listens. If it helps at all, know that I believe you.

PART II

Possible Effects of a Toxic Intimate Relationship

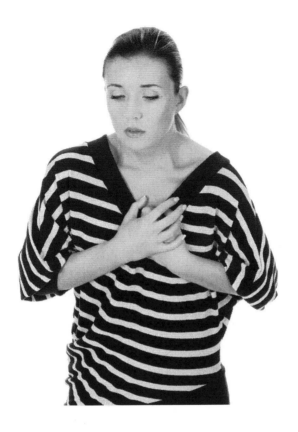

The stress of living with emotional abuse day in and day out puts enormous strain on your mind and body. We all do whatever is necessary to survive, whether it makes sense to others or not. Perhaps you have created a sanctuary for yourself in your mind where you feel safe from the hurtful behavior of your spouse or partner. You detach from the abuse and pretend that it's not really happening. This may work for a while, but eventually your mind and body may rebel and force you to face the truth. That is exactly what happened to me.

The Vacation from Hell

We had looked forward to our family vacation for months. My ex-husband wasn't overly fond of traveling, but I had somehow convinced him that we needed to start making special memories for our daughters. It was only the second family vacation we had ever taken. After months of anticipation, we flew to our vacation destination in August 2007. Our first day of vacation was a lot of fun, but little did I know what lay ahead.

The next day, I started to feel nauseated and dizzy out of the blue. Assuming it was heat stroke, my ex-husband ordered me to sit down. I got up a few minutes later only to grab his arm to stop me from falling. I quickly progressed to total speech loss, body tremors, and confusion. I had no idea what was happening to me.

A fellow tourist who happened to be a registered nurse told my ex-husband that he thought I was having a stroke. I was not yet forty years old. He called 911, and I was taken by ambulance to the nearest hospital. I was asked my name in the emergency room, but I could not remember it without looking at my hospital bracelet. I didn't know who my ex-husband or daughters were. I thought I recognized them from another time in my life but did not make the connection that they were my family.

My speech was slurred and my arms and legs jerked uncontrollably. I thought I was either dying or else I would never walk and speak again. Imagine my surprise when the doctors informed me that after blood tests, an MRI, and a CT scan, they could not find anything medically wrong with me. I was furious! Did they think I was crazy? How does a person make up such sudden and drastic symptoms? I needed it to be something medical because the alternative meant that I had completely lost my mind.

The next day, it started all over again, and so I went back to the hospital. My ex-husband told the staff that they didn't fix me when I spent five hours there the previous day. This statement earned me a ten-hour stay the second time. They ran all the same tests as well as some new ones. I braced myself for a terrible diagnosis. Was it Lyme disease, Bell's palsy, epilepsy, or a stroke? None of the above. Again, medical testing showed nothing physically wrong with me.

At this point, my doctors and nurses asked me if I was experiencing a great deal of stress. I was incredulous. Stress causes an otherwise healthy thirty-nine-year-old woman to physically fall apart? It sounded ridiculous to me.

It's funny how complete strangers could see something I wasn't willing to admit. They asked if my ex-husband and I were getting along. I lied and said that of course we were. They didn't need to know that eighteen months earlier I had uncovered my husband's decades-old secret life of pornography and sexual acting out. They didn't need to know that I was slowly coming to the realization that the man I had been with for fifteen years was severely and pathologically mentally ill—narcissistic personality disorder, to be exact, and that was just for starters. They didn't need to know any of that because I hadn't admitted it to myself yet. I was a Christian, and Christians forgive. I felt a great deal of pressure to forgive him and act like nothing had ever happened, so I tried to do just that.

The rest of our trip I had difficulty walking and speaking. I got severe muscle spasms in my left arm, leg, and neck. It would come and go, seemingly at random. I was still in denial that my "stroke" could be emotionally related, so I refused to go back to the same hospital. I wanted to get home and see my own doctor. She referred me to the local ER, where I was eventually admitted for overnight observation. After more tests and another neurological exam, I was told for the third time that nothing was medically wrong with me. That's when they sent the hospital psychiatrist into my room.

I was faced with yet another stranger who could so plainly see the tension in my marriage that I refused to acknowledge. The psychiatrist repeatedly drove home the point that stress in my marriage was causing my physical symptoms. Finally I relented and told him about discovering my ex-husband's sexual secrets as well as the emotionally abusive behavior he frequently directed at me. I was also experiencing severe anxiety because I was out of work and without health insurance. My ex-husband worked seasonally and refused to carry health insurance for our family. It was the psychiatrist's opinion that the twenty-four/seven time with him during our vacation had triggered severe anxiety that manifested itself in sudden physical symptoms. In psychology, this is referred to as conversion disorder, and its symptoms include

- poor coordination or balance,
- paralysis or weakness,
- difficulty speaking or swallowing,
- retention of urine,
- numbness,
- blindness or other visual symptoms,
- deafness,
- and seizures or convulsions.

Psychological factors, such as stress or conflict, are associated with the appearance of the physical symptoms. Conversion disorder is characterized by one or more symptoms that suggest a neurological condition. It is usually short-lived, although the underlying psychological factors are not. It is imperative to seek counseling after a medical diagnosis is ruled out.

I was floored. Here I thought I had forgiven him and believed the happy facade I put on for everyone else. The thing about our bodies, though, is that we can't lie to them, and mine had finally had enough. I had to face the truth that my ex-husband was not the person he presented to the rest of the world. He was just plain toxic, and I would never get better as long as I stayed with him. Denial is a powerful thing when you are just trying to survive, but conversion disorder was the wake-up call that led me to a new life. It was traumatic and I wouldn't wish it on anyone, but I am also grateful for it. I left for our vacation in good health and came home in a wheelchair and unable to speak. My symptoms were gone within a few days, but that was what it took for me to finally face reality.

Living with Chronic Stress and Anxiety

The example I just described is an extreme physical response to living with someone who is emotionally abusive. It's not something that happens to most people. Usually the stress response is much more subtle. Perhaps you have severe headaches, digestion problems, or physical pain that you or your doctor can't explain. All of these are common ways that the body responds to unrelenting stress. Current research suggests that stress is the root cause of more than 50 percent of physical ailments. While it can feel dismissive for a doctor to write off your physical symptoms as stress, sometimes it's worth careful consideration.

I have given numerous examples of abuse by my ex-husband, but not one of them involves him laying a hand on me. I had no bruises or physical scars. That made it difficult for me to accept that he was anything but a wonderful guy. I tried so hard to believe that, but my mind and body knew better. I was often deeply depressed and couldn't figure out why. The few times we sought help, the focus was typically on my mental health issues. He even took me to the emergency room once and looked liked a very supportive husband for doing so. It just didn't occur to me that I had good reason to be depressed.

I lived in a constant state of anxiety. I never knew what kind of mood to expect, and I was always on guard. It is normal to have a flight-or-fight response when you perceive a threat, but it is not normal for that feeling to never abate. Your body can't tell the different between a threat that is real and one that is perceived. The result can be free-floating anxiety, which is different from fear. Fear is the response to an actual event, whereas anxiety is worry about something that might happen. As I described in trick #1, I often had anxiety attacks at night that kept me from getting a peaceful night's sleep. Chronic fatigue and a feeling of impending doom were also common during my first marriage. If you experience similar symptoms, your body is trying to send you a message you don't want to ignore.

Lingering Effects

When you live with someone who frequently uses emotionally manipulative behavior, you expect everyone else to behave the same way. The abusive behavior feels normal to you. I found this to be true in my own life, even long after my ex and I split up. The best example I can think of is a situation that happened a few months after I met my current husband. We had an extremely minor disagreement about something, and I was sure it would spell doom for our relationship. I wanted to talk about it and sent him an e-mail from work letting him know that. He never answered my e-mail. He also didn't call because he was expecting me to drive up to his house that night. Because he didn't respond to my e-mail or call me, I leapt to the conclusion that he was angry and was giving me the silent treatment. I cried all afternoon. I was deeply saddened by the thought of yet another relationship that had come to this when it had seemed so promising in the beginning.

As it turned out, he had answered my e-mail, but his e-mail server wasn't working properly, and so it never got delivered to me. I found this out when he called me hours later, wondering what was up. I had spent all day crying and berating myself for letting him know I wanted to discuss something. To understand my strange behavior, an observer would have had to know that discussing things openly and honestly in my first marriage was never allowed. Feelings were not allowed either. If I dared to express feelings or initiate a discussion, my ex-husband might have very well given me the silent treatment for days. Even thinking about going through that again was enough to emotionally incapacitate me.

If you have left an emotionally abusive relationship and are in the process of healing, don't be surprised if something like this happens to you.

- When it does (not *if* it does), go easy on yourself and try to see what is really happening.

If you need to relive the experience and grieve for a while, give yourself permission to do so. It hurts to be treated like you don't exist, and you may not have been given permission to experience your emotions in the past. If another person was involved in your trigger experience, be honest with him about what you are experiencing. Hopefully, this person can offer you reassurance that you have done nothing wrong and that he has no intention of treating you like your abuser did.

I was amazed at the difference in our home's atmosphere and the way my body felt the very day my ex moved out. Even at age nine, my youngest daughter verbalized that she could tell the difference. I felt like I could breathe again. I wasn't so nervous all the time, and the unspoken tension vanished from the air. I began to let my guard down and trust people again. Unfortunately, that was not an overnight process. I expected people to hurt me, and it was bewildering to me when they didn't.

When I met Darrell, my current husband, I kept thinking that it was going too well and that nobody could possibly be this kind and decent. Well, at least not to me. I thought I was a hateful person who was embarrassing to be with. The ex's shaming words, tone of voice, and facial expressions kept going through my mind. Darrell helped me realize that they didn't have to be my truth.

- I am a loving person, and I have a lot to offer to those closest to me. It is my ex's problem that he didn't see that, not mine. The same is true for you.
- You can choose to not let your partner destroy your self-esteem.

Dealing with Post Traumatic Stress Disorder after Leaving an Abusive Relationship

It takes a long time to heal from this insidious abuse, and it can be both frustrating and painful. It is not uncommon to move one step forward in your recovery and then get thrown two steps back by something you never saw coming. You may be surprised by how little it can take to trigger a return to those unhappy times, at least in your mind. What can be even more frustrating is to have no idea what sent you back there. Even if you never figure that part out, your emotional and physical reactions will clue you in that your mind and body have gone back in time.

I can usually tell that I have "gone there" when I become weepy or angry, or I feel the discouragement begin to invade my soul until I am headed toward full-blown depression. These episodes are recognizable now because they are so infrequent, but there was a time when I lived like this day in and day out, year after year. The feelings are very familiar, but they don't match my present circumstances.

What I am describing can be labeled a couple different ways, one being triggers and the other being post-traumatic stress disorder. The latter of the two is much more severe, and I haven't had significant enough experience with PTSD to write about it with any authority. However, I do know what it's like to lose a couple of days of my life due to an emotional trigger. I can be in a state of confusion for a while before I figure out what has happened.

After I piece together the clues, I always come back swinging. My ex-husband took sixteen years of my life, and he will not get another minute by messing with my mind—not if I can help it. Although the temptation to lie in bed with the lights out and covers pulled over my head is very great at such times, I do not give into it.

If you're wondering where my strength comes from, I would have to say that the majority of it comes from my faith in God. I believe that he fully intends for me to live a victorious life, one that is free of abuse and in which I can choose to reach my potential. I pray that God will take away my anger and pain and show me what I still need to learn in this trial. My burden is not always released immediately, but it is released.

I also talk about it, a lot, to anyone who will listen. Friends who have known me a long time and know the history of my first marriage can usually offer the best support. Then there are the journals, which are meant for my eyes only, that take the brunt of the emotional vomit.

Most of the time, these coping mechanisms are enough to pull me through a period of reliving the emotional damage I suffered in my previous marriage. If there ever does come a time when I feel stuck, however, I will not hesitate to seek counseling. I will do whatever it takes to live out the promise of John 10:10: "The thief comes only to steal and kill and destroy; I have come that they may have life, and have it to the full."

- Regardless of your faith, know that you are at this point in your life for a reason.

If you have come out of an abusive relationship and survived, there is much for you to learn and to pass on to others. Even if an emotional trigger trips you up, don't let it keep you down. There's a whole new life in front of you.

Should I Stay or Should I Go: The Hardest Decision You May Ever Make

I have shared with you more than a dozen examples of times when my ex-husband behaved in an incredibly abusive manner. It seems like the decision to end the marriage should have been easier than it was, but I never wanted to be divorced and fought hard for my marriage. There is a lot of divorce in my family, and I was sure that I could break the cycle. The last thing in the world I wanted to do was put my children through the pain of divorce. Not that there is ever a "good" age for children to experience the breakup of their parents, but I felt especially guilty that my oldest daughter was twelve years old. Entering the teen years is challenging enough without having to also deal with something as traumatic as your parents' divorce. It wasn't until I was certain that staying would be far more damaging for my daughters than leaving that I finally sought a divorce.

When you're in the process of deciding how to get out of an abusive relationship, it takes all the strength you can muster just to make the decision to leave. You would like to think that the people in your life will support your decision, but that is unfortunately not always the case. This is especially true when the abuse you have suffered is mental and not physical. People can't see your broken heart, your inner turmoil, and your crushing anxiety. They may also be hearing lies about you from your partner, who may act completely innocent while describing you as mentally unbalanced. Whether you decide to leave or stay, you must remain strong and stick to your resolve. No one else has any say in this. Your friends and family can give you their opinions all they want, but they do not lead your life. In this chapter, I discuss some of the things that you may hear if you make the decision to leave.

Blood Is Thicker than Water

You have probably heard the expression "blood is thicker than water," and that can really be true in situations like this. No matter how abusive your partner is, his family and friends will probably refuse to see it. While it hurts to be misunderstood, it is understandable in this case. A loyalty line has been drawn, and you're on the other side of it.

What can really throw you for a loop is when mutual friends don't believe you or question your true motives for leaving. Suddenly, the person who has made your life a living hell for years is a saint in the eyes of these people.

At times like these, you must make the decision to cut your losses and move on. People who judge you without hearing your side of the story probably aren't worth holding onto anyway.

How Can You Call It Abuse When He Has Never Hit You?

Emotional abuse can take on many different forms, including narcissism, giving the silent treatment, playing the victim, projection, manipulation, verbal abuse, constant passive-aggressive behavior, overly controlling behavior, talking down to you, gaslighting, rewriting history, playing dumb, spreading lies about you, and so many more. Over time these behaviors can wear you down and make you feel like you are losing your mind.

If someone you care about makes this statement to you, you have a few choices in how to respond. One is to get angry and defend yourself, and the other is to laugh in the other person's face. Your "concerned friend" or family member obviously has no idea when it comes to the reality of your life, and you are under no obligation to convince him or her that your abuse is real. You know the truth and that is all that matters.

People Give Up Too Easily on Marriage These Days

This is one of those statements that send me into next week. I don't personally know of anyone who woke up one day and decided that being married wasn't all that much fun anymore. Without fail, the marriages I know that have ended in divorce all involved abuse, addiction, adultery, or abandonment. Every relationship goes through ups and downs, and the partners have their petty annoyances with each other, but marriages that fall into the "Four A's," as I call them, are an entirely different situation.

Most people who use this line do so with a judgmental tone and a "tsk, tsk, tsk" on their lips. They will encourage you to try marriage counseling, as if you had never considered that idea. Unfortunately, when one-half of the couple relies on abusive behavior to get his own way, counseling doesn't work out too well. The emotionally abusive person will say what the counselor wants to hear and may turn things around so it looks like you are causing all the problems. When you have to make the excruciating decision to end a marriage, the only people who deserve an explanation are your children. Even then it needs to be age-appropriate.

Unhelpful Things Religious People Said when I Got Divorced

If you belong to a faith community, you can probably expect a fair amount of pushback. That is where most of mine came from. My family and friends had been exposed to my ex enough to see the kind of person he really was. Our church family did not. They only saw the Sunday ex, the one who acted like an attentive husband and father for sixty minutes a week. Here are some of the more memorable comments and my responses to them.

God hates divorce. I know he does, but I have also come to believe that he loves me more than he hates divorce. He does not want to see me disrespected, and continued abuse kept me from knowing his will for my life. I know this may be a controversial thing to say, but I feel that some of the more conservative denominations of the Christian church have made an idol out of marriage. Abused women are told to stay and be more submissive. They are made responsible for their husband's relationship with God. I questioned the kind of God who cared more about my incredibly unhealthy marriage than he did about me as an individual.

The church is one of the worst offenders when it comes to making judgmental, unhelpful remarks. It's as though marriages must stay together regardless of the cost to the abused spouse and children. I'm not saying that the church should encourage divorce, but it should be willing to look at each situation individually and recognize when abuse is taking place. The abuser should then be held responsible for changing his behavior. What usually happens is that the spouse who makes claims of abusive behavior is silenced, judged, and shamed, and the abusive person's behavior only escalates.

You can only change yourself. I am fully aware of this, and I believe it myself. I think this was along the lines of how I chose to respond to my ex-husband. I could choose love and forgiveness no matter how he behaved. To me, enabling someone's poor behavior and choices is not love. When there are no consequences, it's almost guaranteed that things will get worse. Many churches today do not have a realistic sense of personal boundaries.

You allowed yourself to get sick (with the neurological symptoms that were stress-related). Words can't do justice to how judged and shamed I felt upon hearing this statement. I left the room in tears, never to return to this so-called spiritual mentor again.

Your relationship with God must not have been strong enough. And you know this how?

Another person can't mentally or emotionally abuse you unless you allow it. I was so stunned by this statement that I couldn't speak. I thought I was supposed to allow his abuse and just pray for him. Wouldn't not allowing him to abuse me be playing God?

Do you really want your children to grow up with divorced parents like you did? Of course I didn't want that! I thought I had married a devoted Christian who would always treat me well. Many women get married under the illusion that they will start a family and everyone will live happily ever after. When children enter a marriage, the commitment to stay together usually gets even stronger. If you have to seek a divorce to protect your children from mental abuse, it is not you who broke up the family: it is the partner who chose to be so unloving in the first place. People who want to see you remain stuck use this line to produce intense guilt because it works. What mother wants to think she broke up her family for what someone else may see as frivolous reasons?

God will perform a miracle, just keep praying and waiting. I know God can and does perform miracles every day. For a few years, I thought our marriage was one. I so wanted to be one of the few marriages that survive the kind of betrayal and abuse that I experienced. I was told to try harder, pray more, love more, forgive more, and exclude everyone from my life who criticized my ex. I must never try to change him or share personal things about him with others. Outside of Christian circles, the behavior I was encouraged to adopt is called codependency.

You need to make yourself more physically attractive to him. No one can argue that I am not both significantly overweight and out of style, but it would not have mattered if I had been a Victoria's Secret model. My ex-husband is a sexual addict with desires no human can satisfy.

You need to plan for how you are going to handle it if he relapses into his pornography addiction…without leaving him. It is wrong to pu

away money or plan for an education (in other words, a Plan B) because that is not trusting God enough. My only response to this was stunned silence. It seemed like my spiritual mentor would go to any lengths to justify my ex's behavior and put me in my place.

You're making a mountain out of a molehill. Is there any more dismissive statement than this? I heard this several times about my ex's pornography addiction. He's a man, that's how men are wired, blah blah blah. I want to set the record straight and let you know that I use the word "pornography" very loosely here. His sexual addiction was actually much more deviant in nature, but I don't feel that specifics are necessary. I have no idea why people feel the need to dismiss others' experiences or pain. "You think that's bad, what about what Susie Jones went through, and you didn't see her getting divorced." Good for Susie Jones. That's her decision, and really none of anyone else's business.

Consider Their Motives

For some reason, people who have never given you grief before feel the need to meddle when it's evident that a relationship is failing beyond repair. It's hard to know what their motives are. Sometimes it is a genuine desire to be helpful, and the words don't come out quite right. More often than not, there is a hidden agenda that has very little to do with you.

If the person who is making these kinds of statements to you is also in an abusive relationship, your actions may be very threatening. It is like you are holding up a mirror and forcing him or her to face a reality he or she doesn't want to face. By trying to convince you to stay with an abuser, he or she is more than likely trying to convince him- or herself. Another possibility is that your accuser is also an abuser and doesn't like for you to use the word "abuse" to describe his or her own behavior.

And then there are those legalistic religious folks who believe that you should never divorce, no matter what.

- Your best response to this is to tell them that if they are against divorce, don't get one.

It's your life to live, and the sooner you sever ties with those who want to hold you down, the sooner you can start over and heal from the abuse.

After the Decision Is Made

As difficult as it is to identify your partner's behavior as abusive, it is only the first step. You then have to decide what you are going to do about it. Most people don't leap immediately from naming the abusive behavior to ending the relationship. If you're not married or don't have children together, there is less at stake. However, legal binds and/or children in common make it a whole different ball game.

There were about five years between the time I first knew my marriage was in serious trouble to the time I decided to end it. Throughout that duration, I was firmly committed to keeping the marriage together. There was nothing I wouldn't have done in order to make that happen. I understand the desire and I never judge people for giving it their all, even when the other person clearly isn't doing the same thing. I don't think anyone should end a relationship that involves children if there is any way at all that it could work out. You need to get to that sense of peace about letting go that I finally arrived at in late 2008. If you don't, you will always wonder what could have been. By the time I divorced, I had no doubts remaining.

- All of this being said, I feel the most important thing to remember is that you can't change your partner.

You haven't had his life experiences and can't begin to understand what drives his behavior. When my first marriage was clearly unraveling, I became obsessed with trying to understand my ex. I thought if I knew everything about his formative years then I would understand why he acted the way he did. Unfortunately, I crossed a lot of personal boundaries in my quest for this information. I thought there simply had to be an explanation for the way he was. To not get an answer meant that my emotional turmoil was in vain. The truth is there is no way to fully understand another person. If you can accept that, it may be possible to detach from his behavior and take it less personally.

I recommend that you work with a counselor who is skilled in helping you establish boundaries in your relationship. It's true that you can only change yourself, even if that sounds trite. If you decide to stay, you need to focus on changing the way you react to your partner's manipulative behavior. You may resent the effort you are making and it may ultimately have no effect on your relationship, but you won't know unless your try. Of course, you should be prepared to leave immediately if your partner threatens you or your children or if you ever feel unsafe.

I recently read a quote on Facebook that sums up what I am trying to say here very well: "One of the hardest decisions you will ever face in life is choosing whether to walk away or try harder." I wish you peace with your decision. It is one that only you can make.

My Marriage Is Over, So Why Do I Feel Like a Tossed Salad?

Many women who leave an emotionally abusive relationship are surprised by the intensity of their conflicting emotions once they are finally free of the person who caused them so much pain. It can feel like someone put the ingredients for a salad into a bag, shook it up, dumped it all over the floor, and left you to deal with the mess. While feeling mixed-up and confused aren't particularly pleasant emotions to experience, they are perfectly normal and—believe it or not—also healthy and necessary. I have been there myself and am here to tell you that your emotions eventually settle down.

Shouldn't Getting Divorced Make Me Feel Sad?

I will always remember the feeling of immense relief I had when my ex-husband finally moved out of our home, even though it meant that I had to take care of the house and two kids by myself. It was actually less of a burden than feeling like I had three kids, one of whom happened to be an extremely immature, fully-grown man. I also felt very happy, an emotion I hadn't experienced in years and didn't quite know how to handle. My daughters, ages twelve and nine at the time, seemed to experience the same initial sense of relief that I did even though they were sad that the family had finally come to this.

Repressed Emotions Can Blow Up in Your Face

My ex-husband was manipulative, passive-aggressive, angry, narcissistic, and he lived in a fantasy world with his sexual addiction. I can say that now, but I sure couldn't say it then. Instead, he told me that there was nothing wrong with him and that if I thought there was, it only meant there was something wrong with me. This sentiment was often reinforced by people in my faith community who were trying to help me keep my marriage together. My immediate family and close friends could see my reality, but I denied it in order to survive. Feelings were absolutely forbidden in my first marriage.

After thirteen years of living in an alternate reality, I was liberated when he left. While the awful, unspoken tension was gone and my daughters and I could relax, the happy and relieved feelings were not the only ones we experienced. Those initial feelings were only the beginning of a roller coaster of emotions that I rode for about the next year.

I never cried after the divorce finally went through because I was no longer distraught about it. After all the crying I had done during my marriage, I just felt flat and had no more tears left. I did question whether or not I had given the marriage a fair chance, despite the fact that I had remained married years longer than most people would have under similar circumstances. I also felt tremendous guilt because I was no longer willing to excuse my ex's behavior or try to love him enough to finally "fix" him. It was very difficult to give up the idea that if I just tried harder and loved him unconditionally, whatever damage he had within him would heal. If it didn't happen after sixteen years together, it was never going to happen.

The one emotion that knocked my socks off was my anger. Actually, anger is an understatement. What I felt toward my ex-husband was absolute rage. Rage that I had been lied to for years, rage that he didn't appreciate my love, rage that I had given him sixteen years of my life only to be tossed aside like an old shoe. I am a fairly mild-mannered person and when I realized that I had the capacity for so much rage inside of me, it frightened me terribly. That alone was enough to make me realize how terribly unhealthy my first marriage was.

What Can You Expect?

Naturally, every person in an abusive relationship is different and had different experiences that led up to her leaving. According to the London Abused Women's Centre, you may experience some, all, or none of the following emotions, sometimes on the same day. Since I have already touched on anger and elation, I won't go over those again.

Grief. You have experienced a loss that is as real as a death: the loss of your marriage or relationship and all the dreams that went with it. If you were physically or emotionally abused, you may be hard on yourself for feeling grief over the loss of your relationship, but you shouldn't be. There were probably some good times, even if they were infrequent, and you may miss what once was. The memories of the good times are probably what kept you hanging on for so long.

Feeling like a failure. Even if leaving was the best possible decision for you and your children, you may still struggle with the feeling that you are a personal failure because your relationship ended. If you are like me, you did everything in your power to hold things together, and the marriage fell apart because the abusive person was simply unwilling to change. That's on them, not you.

Anxiety. Learning to live a normal life without the constant fear of upsetting the abusive person in your life takes some getting used to. Even though it is healthy, it is unknown, and people tend to fear what they don't know. Remind yourself that it is normal to feel scared but that you made the right decision and are moving in the right direction.

Feeling disoriented. Time and distance from relationships tend to change our perspective, and you may feel totally dazed and out of it for a while. If you are dealing with memories that have been repressed for a long time, you may question your own sanity and wonder if those things really happened. It can be a strange feeling to suddenly see your former partner as he really is and not how you projected him to be for all those years in order to remain in the relationship.

Feeling lonely. When your relationship ended, it also changed several other relationships at the same time. If you were once close to your in-laws, it can be devastating if they suddenly want nothing to do with you. If you had children with your partner, you could feel lonely when they are spending time with him. Although it can be tempting to give in to loneliness and start to withdraw, it isn't healthy in the long run. This is a perfect time to cultivate new interests and friendships.

Wanting to get back together. When the process of recovery becomes too much to bear, it can be tempting to want to reconcile with your abusive partner just so you don't have to deal with the pain of being on your own anymore. At times like these, remind yourself of why you left and whether being back together would really be better than the temporary intensity of emotions that you are presently experiencing.

Starting Your New Life

One of the reasons that the months immediately following divorce or separation can be so painful is that you must come to identify yourself in a whole new way. When my marriage ended, I literally had no idea who I was. I had looked to him to identify me for so long that I didn't recognize the person I was left with when he was no longer there. It was terrifying and thrilling all at the same time.

This can be a time of really getting to know yourself, and it actually can be very exciting. Without an abusive person there to sensor your emotions and stifle your creativity, you may discover characteristics about yourself that you had long since forgotten. I discovered that I have a good sense of humor and enjoy making others laugh. I also rediscovered my faith without being limited to what my ex-husband believed. Perhaps the greatest thing I found hidden in myself is that I still like to write, just as I did when I was a little girl.

New Relationships

Most abuse counselors recommend that you wait at least a year before dating again, just so you have given yourself enough time to work through the emotions of your last relationship. I was two months shy of that, but my story has a happy ending because I married the first man I dated post-divorce. We got married in July 2010, and we couldn't be happier. You know yourself, and you will know when you feel ready, so just be sure to give yourself some time and take it from there.

One thing to be aware of when entering new relationships is that they may trigger memories of the old one. This was something I couldn't understand because my second husband has no abusive tendencies, and the triggering didn't always seem to have a context. Like the other emotions that have been discussed, having a sudden memory of abuse doesn't have to make logical sense, and it probably won't. The important thing is that you acknowledge it, process what has come to your mind, and move on with your new and healthy life as soon as possible.

I Leave You with Hope

If I had remained in my first marriage, I shudder to think of what life would be like today for my daughters and me. Even though letting go of it was the hardest thing I have ever done in my life, I have been abundantly blessed since that time. I went from bankruptcy and despair to a comfortable, happy life. I credit my faith with much of it. I let go and placed everything in God's hands. I still can't get over how much our lives have changed in such a short amount of time. The year between my first marriage ending and meeting my second husband was both challenging and wonderful. I found strength that I never knew I had and started my life over again at the age of forty.

By far the greatest blessing has been meeting and marrying Darrell. How someone so kind, humble, and self-sacrificing remained single into his mid forties is beyond me. I like to call him the anti-narcissist. I don't think the man has ever put himself first. To go from being treated with disdain and contempt to being truly loved and cherished is such an amazing feeling that it's nearly indescribable. I know not everyone gets this lucky or even has the desire to get into another relationship. I am just here to tell you that you deserve the same kind of love and respect I found. When you take the time to heal and really know yourself, you won't attract the same type of person into your life again. Life beyond abuse is a beautiful thing.

Printed in Great Britain
by Amazon.co.uk, Ltd.,
Marston Gate.